THE DOGS of NEWTOWN

Guy A. Bacon

I dedicate this book to my sister,
Charlotte Helen Bacon.

I would like to thank my teacher Ms. King
for helping me through this long process.
Also, I would like to thank Mary Bloom
for the photography, Sandy Cornell for our friendship,
and ALL of the therapy dogs that
visited Reed Intermediate School.

INTRODUCTION

Newtown, CT, has struggled since December of 2012, but the sadness in Newtown has gotten a little bit better because of therapy dogs that came to visit from around America. My life has gotten better because of these therapy dogs.

My name is Guy Bacon and I am 11 years old. I am a student at Reed Intermediate School (RIS) in Newtown, CT. This book is about some of the most special therapy dogs that visited me and my friends at school and helped lick the tears away from our faces.

I was surprised to see the dogs on the first day of school in January, 2013. I remember that I was standing in front of my desk when Drago walked into our classroom. He was the first dog that I saw and got to pet. I felt very calm and relaxed whenever I touched any of the dogs' soft, fluffy fur. They also made me very comfortable when they would lick and nuzzle me back.

FOREWORD

In the days immediately following the events of 12/14, Newtown teachers, and administrators wanted nothing more than to help our students feel safe coming back to school. There is no teacher guide for this situation, and we were feeling the same sadness, fear and confusion as our students.

Thankfully, we were not on our own. With the teachers in the school hallways those first mornings were about ten comfort dogs and their steady, generous, volunteer owners. They stood among us as the first students headed our way. *"There are dogs in school!"* were the first words I heard, and a hundred little hands reached out to touch, pet, hug, or cuddle a dog. And then the flood of questions began – How old? What breed? What's his name? Blessedly, for all of us, these were questions that could be answered. The dogs and their owners spent every day for the rest of the school year in service to the staff and students of our school. They became a welcomed distraction, a calming presence, a hug waiting to happen. Not only did the students and staff seek out these dogs, but the dogs seemed to have an uncanny ability to find those who needed them most. For us, they were unconditional love. They were friends that did not require words, and yet somehow understood the words that could not be spoken. These gentle dogs, and their owners, became part of our Reed family that year.

For a while I walked around saying, "Someone should write a book about these dogs." And, thankfully, Guy Bacon decided to do just that. His first days back at school were spent sitting, kneeling or sometimes lying next to a dog - his notebook open, his pencil poised, his tongue curled over his lip and his brows furrowed in concentration as he conducted interview after interview with comfort dogs of all sizes and breeds. This was time well spent. The dogs were a special gift for Guy, just as he was for them. And this book is the product of those long, snuggle-filled interview sessions, and the mutual love that was, and still is, shared by Guy and the dogs of Newtown.

Karen King

DRAGO was Ms. King's first read-aloud dog, and he made us feel calm. Ms. King was my 5th-grade teacher at RIS. Drago has a big stuffed toy moose.

SIENA also came to visit. She and Drago have the same owner. Siena likes to chew Elk antlers.

Both dogs have earned obedience rally, retriever and pointing titles! Besides RIS, Drago and Siena also visit friends at other schools, VA Hospitals and libraries. Both Drago and Siena like helping people to feel better, if only for a short period of time. They believe that making a difference is something every dog can do in a small way.

KONA is a two-year-old female Boston Terrier. She likes to give kisses and get hugs and belly scratches in return. One special thing about Kona is that she knows how to ride a skateboard. She also knows how to press a "No" button.

Kona likes to do other tricks and play with her Greyhound stepsisters. Kona loves to eat anything (food). Her two favorite things to do are taking naps in the sun and coming to see the kids at RIS. Kona's favorite toy is a dental dinosaur. Kona visits the STARR room often, a place in school where teachers help kids at school with disabilities.

Besides RIS, Kona enjoys visiting friends at other schools and libraries. She loves seeing the joy on the children's and adults' faces. But most of all her favorite thing about being a visiting dog is seeing me!

NESSA is a female Pembroke Welsh Corgi. This gentle dog likes to give kisses and cuddle. Nessa's favorite toy is a ball. She is in the group called Agility, where she practices on an obstacle course. She runs really, really fast - even faster than me. Nessa likes to play with her brother and sister, and especially enjoys going to the beach. Nessa loves the snow, as long as it is not over her head. Nessa likes Reed Intermediate School and the kids here. What I like about Nessa is that she is small, but mighty at the same time.

ANNIE is a five-year-old female Beagle mix. She loves food and kids, and enjoys getting treats out of her Kong toy. Annie always does tricks for treats. Annie's favorite trick is "sit up". Just like Kona, Annie loves going to STARR. Annie was a rescue dog from Kentucky, and was about 8 months old when she was adopted from Danbury Animal Welfare Society (DAWS). She took training classes so she could be the perfect therapy dog. She loves to see everyone and make sure she says hello with her wagging tail. Annie also visits first graders who read to her along with people who are in hospitals and nursing homes. She goes room to room making it a happy and lively place.

KIPPER is a six-year-old Rough Collie who lives in Bethel. Kipper loves people, especially children. He enjoys being hugged and pet. Kipper likes to sit and work on rawhide chews. Kipper also likes to lie down in the warm sun at school. Kipper enjoys going to Peachwave to be treated to some tasty vanilla frozen yogurt. Kipper likes dog practice; and he also likes me. He visits RIS, special education classrooms and a memory care unit. He is special because he is like a sensei. He is wise and always chooses the people who need him most.

YANKEE is a male Labradoodle. Yankee loves squeaky toys and playing hide-and-seek. His favorite toy is a blue Frisbee. Yankee loves to ride in the car and to come to school. Yankee has chicken-flavored toothpaste. He visits elementary schools to help kids read, and also nursing homes. Yankee likes spreading happiness because it makes him happy too.

DAISY is a female Golden Retriever whose favorite toy is a Kong. Daisy likes to run around outside chasing squirrels. When she is not playing with her sister, Stella, Daisy likes to take naps on the couch.

Sketch by Guy. In loving
memory of Daisy.

She loves coming to school. Daisy loves coming to
read-aloud when she can plop right on the floor with all
the kids. Sadly, Daisy passed away in April of 2015.
We will miss her.

WALLACE is a four-year-old Labrador Retriever who loves being pet and having his belly scratched. Wallace likes to run and chase a ball. A Nylabone is Wallace's favorite toy. Wallace likes to eat apples, carrots and celery. Wallace was born in Scotland and came to the United States on an airplane. He was supposed to be trained to hunt birds but he wasn't sure that's what he wanted to do. Wallace became a therapy dog instead. He is a very good therapy dog. Besides RIS, Wallace visits kindergarten classes so that children can read to him. His favorite thing about being a therapy dog is seeing the smiles on everyone's faces.

SPARTACUS is a huge four-year-old American Akita. Spartacus likes racket balls. Spartacus likes rides in the car, and he especially likes taking trips to the beach. Spartacus loves to play in the snow too. He visits hospitals, schools and helps people in their time of need. He likes seeing people smile when he trots into the room.

DAISY is a female Leonberger. She is very nice and goes crazy when somebody goes crazy about her. She loves to be pet in a special spot around her right leg. When you scratch her there, she starts to kick! Daisy likes kids and also likes to swim. She enjoys exploring and looking for things to play with in the house. Daisy likes ice cubes, and likes to bark (Woof!) at the freezer. Daisy likes the car. Daisy likes every dog she meets (especially her friend, Kona) and also likes birds. Daisy belongs to her handler's son. Daisy is honored to be in our book. She does home and school visits, and loves the smiles and hugs she gets.

WINSTON is a seven-year-old black Labrador who loves read-aloud time. Winston put a dog print on a classmate's get-well card. Winston likes dog treats, food, swimming, hikes, and enjoys being pet. He has a sister named Diva. Winston loves the winter snow. Winston also likes trips to the beach in the summer.

Winston has fur and he sheds. He likes to go for walks or rides in the car. Winston also visits assisted living facilities, spending time with residents who tell him about dogs they had when they were younger. His favorite thing about being a therapy dog is seeing people's eyes light up when they see him.

RUBY is a seven-year-old female Boxer. Ruby looks a little scary, but she is really a very gentle and friendly dog. Ruby likes kids and dogs and cats. Ruby loves any toy that squeaks when she bites it. Ruby loves to be with the kids in STARR. Ruby visits patients at hospitals and cancer centers. Recently, she visited a stroke patient who didn't talk. When Ruby came in the room, he said, "I love dogs!". Ruby was happy to help the patient and make the patient's daughter smile too. Like Daisy, Ruby passed away. We will never forget you Ruby. Rest in Peace.

Sketch by Guy.
In loving memory
of Ruby.

SKYLAR is a four year old male Golden Retriever with nine brothers and sisters. Skylar likes to run and fetch the ball with children. He loves to get together to play with his six buddies every night at 7 PM. Skylar loves going to the library, and enjoys every single read-aloud story. He loves to give kisses and also get hugs in return. Skylar has his own reading program called, "Read with Skylar". He also helps first responders and their families. His favorite thing about being a therapy dog is seeing the happiness he brings - especially to children.

ARWEN is a champion Siberian Husky and sometimes works as a model. She has very thick and soft fur. She has two different colored eyes, blue and brown. Arwen sheds a lot. No need for hair cuts! Arwen was one of my favorites, but sadly she passed away in late April 2014. Since then, her grandson, Ringo, and granddaughter, Rumor, have stepped in to fill her big paws and carry on the family tradition of helping people.

GB
6/15

Sketch by Guy. In loving memory of Arwen.

CONCLUSION

These dogs are just a sample of the many therapy dogs who came to Reed Intermediate School. All of the dogs helped me feel a lot better, and also made all of the other students feel better, too. I felt safer with them here. The dogs' handlers gave us trading cards, each with the dog's picture on it. We collected these, and they are a good way of remembering all of the dogs. These dogs are our friends. I felt sad when the dogs left, and I'm guessing the other kids did too. They made it easier for me to go to school. But why were they here? They were here to help us, and they did.

Charlotte's Litter, Inc.

Copyright © 2015 by Guy A. Bacon

ISBN: 978-0-9863001-2-7

Visit our website at www.gooddogsgreatlisteners.com

Printed in the United States of America.